MW00364945

SCHADEN-FREEZERS!

56 CRUEL JOKES IN 12 FUN FLAVORS!

SCHADEN·FREEZERS!

JASON KREHER • MATT MOORE

FOREWORD BY ANTHONY JESELNIK
PHOTOGRAPHY BY RAY GORDON

Adamsmedia
Avon, Massachusetts

Published by
Adams Media, a division of F+W Media, Inc.
57 Littlefield Street, Avon, MA 02322. U.S.A.
www.adamsmedia.com

ISBN 10: 1-4405-8520-2
ISBN 13: 978-1-4405-8520-3
eISBN 10: 1-4405-8521-0
eISBN 13: 978-1-4405-8521-0

Printed in China.

10   9   8   7   6   5   4   3   2   1

Photography by Ray Gordon.
Cover design by Matt Moore & Jason Kreher.

This book is available at quantity discounts for bulk purchases.
For information, please call 1-800-289-0963.

He who eats alone chokes alone.

~Proverb

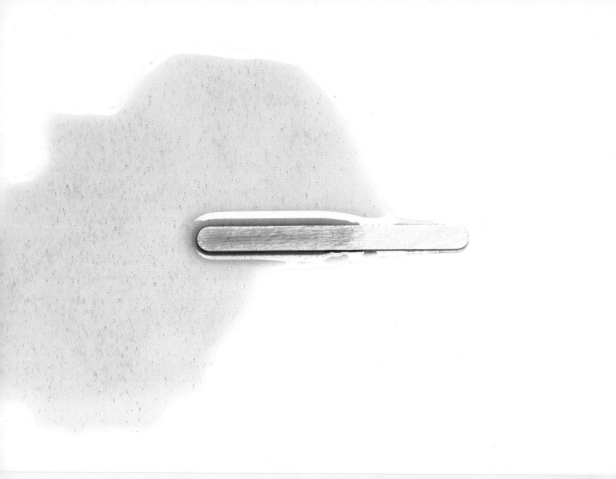

ACKNOWLEDGMENTS

This book could not have happened without the talent and efforts of many. Jason and Matt would like to thank the following people, each of whom contributed something vital to the process:

Matt Sorrell, Jason Roark, Emily Fincher, Smith Henderson, Duvall Osteen, Tom Hardej and the good people at Adams Media, Wieden + Kennedy, Anthony Jeselnik, Ray Gordon, Ben Sellon, Food Chain Films, Rob Kendall, Margo Latka, Eirik Anderson, and God.

Matt would also like to formally apologize to his mother, Leisa Whitacre Moore.

FOREWORD

Jokes are fragile contraptions. The setup must be built to hold the weight of the punch line, and the punch line must be heavy enough that the setup balances logically. Don't worry if this explanation is confusing to you. I'm a comedic genius, and you're just some poor bastard reading a book about Popsicle sticks.

Jokes must be told properly. If brevity and timing weren't impor-tant, the greatest comedians of all time would be our mothers. That's what makes this book so great. The jokes are hilarious, but only in the context provided on the page. You have to see the Popsicle stick in order laugh at the joke. It's not just seeing the words, printed in the tiny font of our childhood summers. It's the colorful stain over the punch line that really makes me happy. I cannot read these jokes without imagining an innocent child, sweating through a hot day on the jungle gym, excitedly unwrapping a frozen treat.

In a rare display of patience, the child studies the dessert's handle, careful to keep his fingers dry: **WHAT DID THE GRANDMA SAY TO THE FROG?** He does not know. The child begins to enjoy the Popsicle—eating carefully at first, with concern for sharp headaches. But after a minute or two he is devouring the pop as fast as he can, until only stained fingers and a piece of wood are left.

By the time the playground beckons once again, the child remembers there is a story written on his garbage. He rechecks the forgotten setup: **WHAT DID THE GRANDMA SAY TO THE FROG?** He thinks for a second—has he heard this one before? No. He's almost grinning in anticipation as he looks to the punch line: **SOMETHING RACIST, PROBABLY.**

He'll have to ask his mom what this one means. The conversation will not end well.

Jason Kreher and Matt Moore just ruined some kid's whole summer. Whole childhood, probably.

Hilarious.

—ANTHONY JESELNIK

INTRODUCTION

Think back on some of your fondest memories from childhood. Chances are, food was part of at least a few special moments—a cloud of pink cotton candy at your first baseball game; the pack of Sixlets your dad bought for you when he lost his job; an ice cream cone you shared with your grandpa just before he poisoned all those dogs. There are plenty of special treats that can transport us back to a happier time, but if you ask us, nothing in the world beats a good old-fashioned Popsicle.

What could be better on a hot July day? A colorful, icy treat with a built-in gag to share with your pals. Sure, the jokes could get a little corny. But as an innocent kid, those puns were just about the funniest dang thing on earth. Sometimes you'd even laugh so hard that you'd forget about your sister's diagnosis. Now that's a real belly laugh!

Humor is a funny thing—a joke that makes you laugh might be considered "offensive" by someone else, while something that really upsets you might bring other people a lot of joy. Especially if they're German. There are all sorts of things that have the power to make people happy, whether it's a clown making a silly face, a funny rhyme about animals, or a mentally ill person yelling on a street corner. Ha ha! What is he even saying?! It makes us smile just thinking about it.

And I guess that's why we wrote this book in the first place. To tickle your tummy with a few silly jokes, and to remind you that we are all just fragile bags of meat and water who will most certainly die.

We love you, and we hope you enjoy the book.

—JASON & MATT

Schadenfreude: *noun*
scha·den·freu·de [SHä′dənfroid′ə]
pleasure derived from another person's misfortune
ORIGIN: German, from *Schaden,* 'harm,' + *Freude,* 'joy'

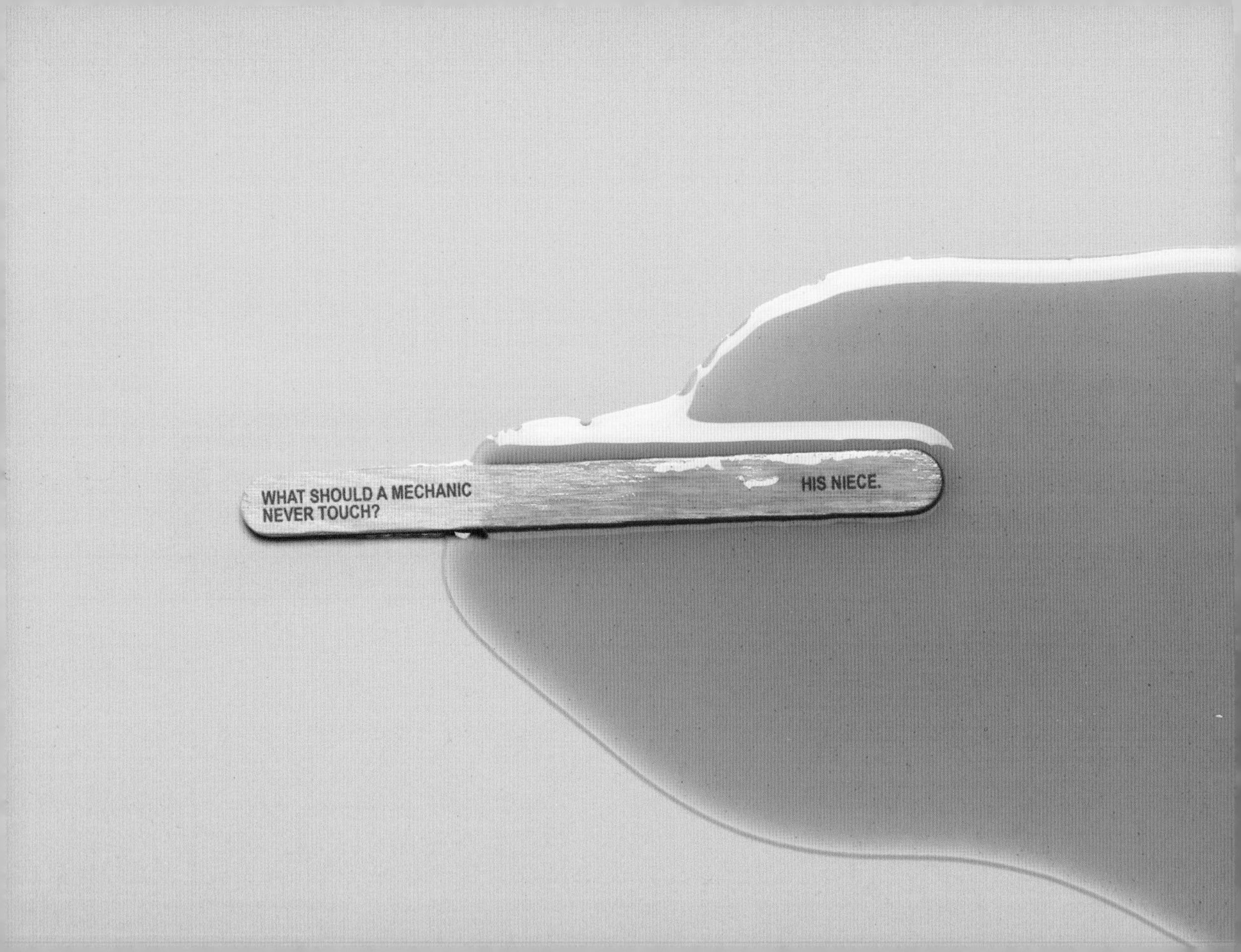
WHAT SHOULD A MECHANIC
NEVER TOUCH?
HIS NIECE.

WHY WAS THE ELEPHANT RED?

WHY WAS THE ELEPHANT RED?

SOMEBODY TOOK HER IVORY!

WHAT MAKES A JANITOR HAPPY?

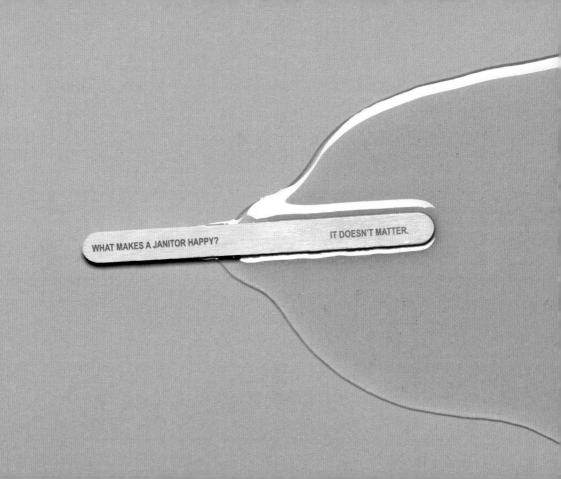

WHAT'D THE BELL SAY TO THE BRIDESMAID?

WHAT'D THE BELL SAY TO THE BRIDESMAID?

"I GIVE IT 8 MONTHS."

WHY WAS THE BUTTERFLY SLEEPY?   LUPUS.

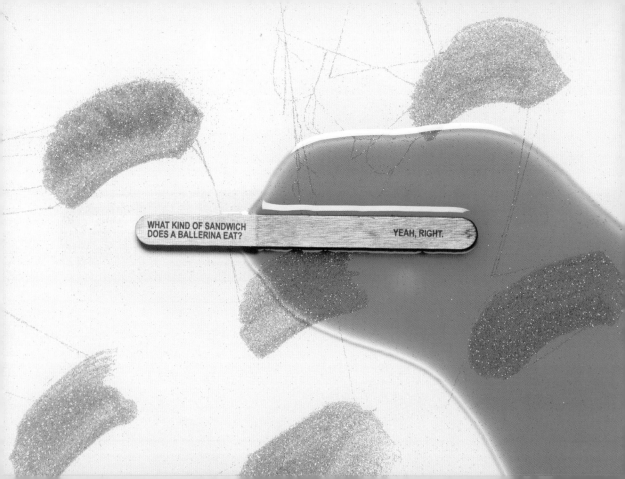

WHY DID THE EARTHQUAKE'S
PARENTS SPLIT UP?

WHY DID THE EARTHQUAKE'S
PARENTS SPLIT UP?

IT WAS HER "FAULT."

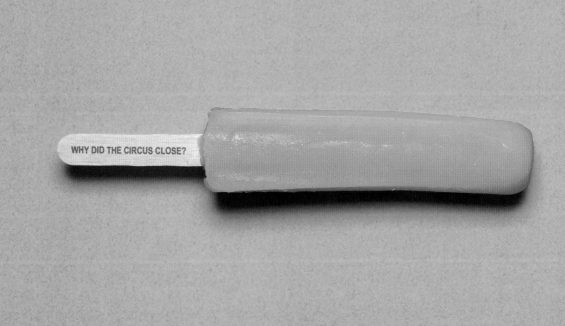

WHY DID THE CIRCUS CLOSE?

A LONG, CHILLING LIST OF
ANIMAL RIGHTS VIOLATIONS.

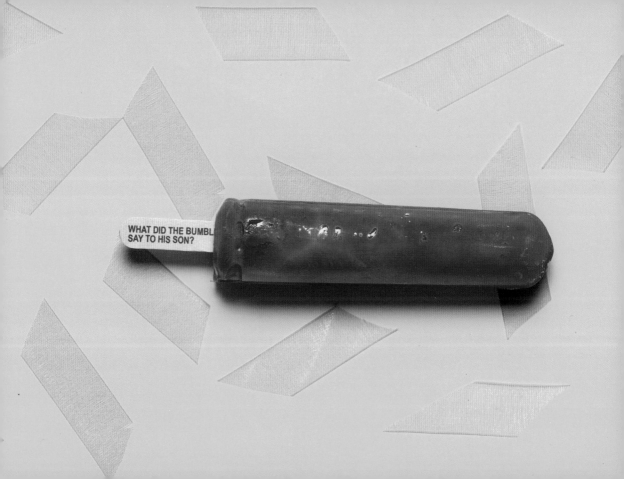

WHAT DID THE BUMBLEBEE
SAY TO HIS SON?

"EVERY OTHER WEEKEND ISN'T
SO BAD. RIGHT PAL?"

WHAT DID THE JUDGE SAY
TO THE BASEBALL PLAYER?

WHAT DID THE JUDGE SAY
TO THE BASEBALL PLAYER?

"CHILD SUPPORT IS NOT
OPTIONAL, MR. SANDERS."

WHAT DID THE LION
DO AFTER SCHOOL?

WHAT DID THE LION
DO AFTER SCHOOL?

LOOKED FOR WORK FOR A WHILE,
AND THEN SORT OF GAVE UP.

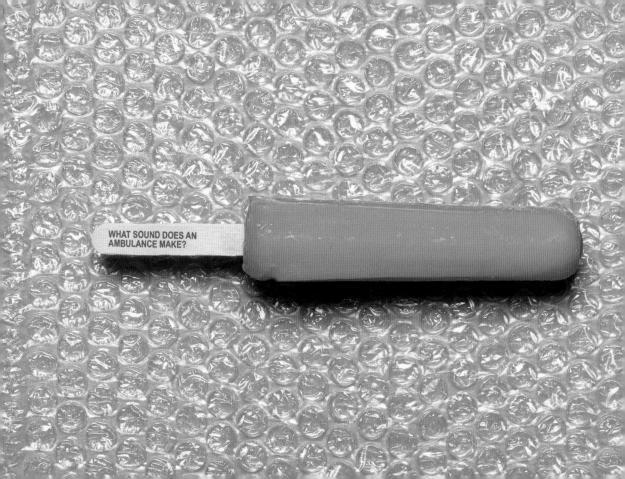

WHAT SOUND DOES AN
AMBULANCE MAKE?

NONE, ONCE THE SIRENS ARE TURNED OFF.

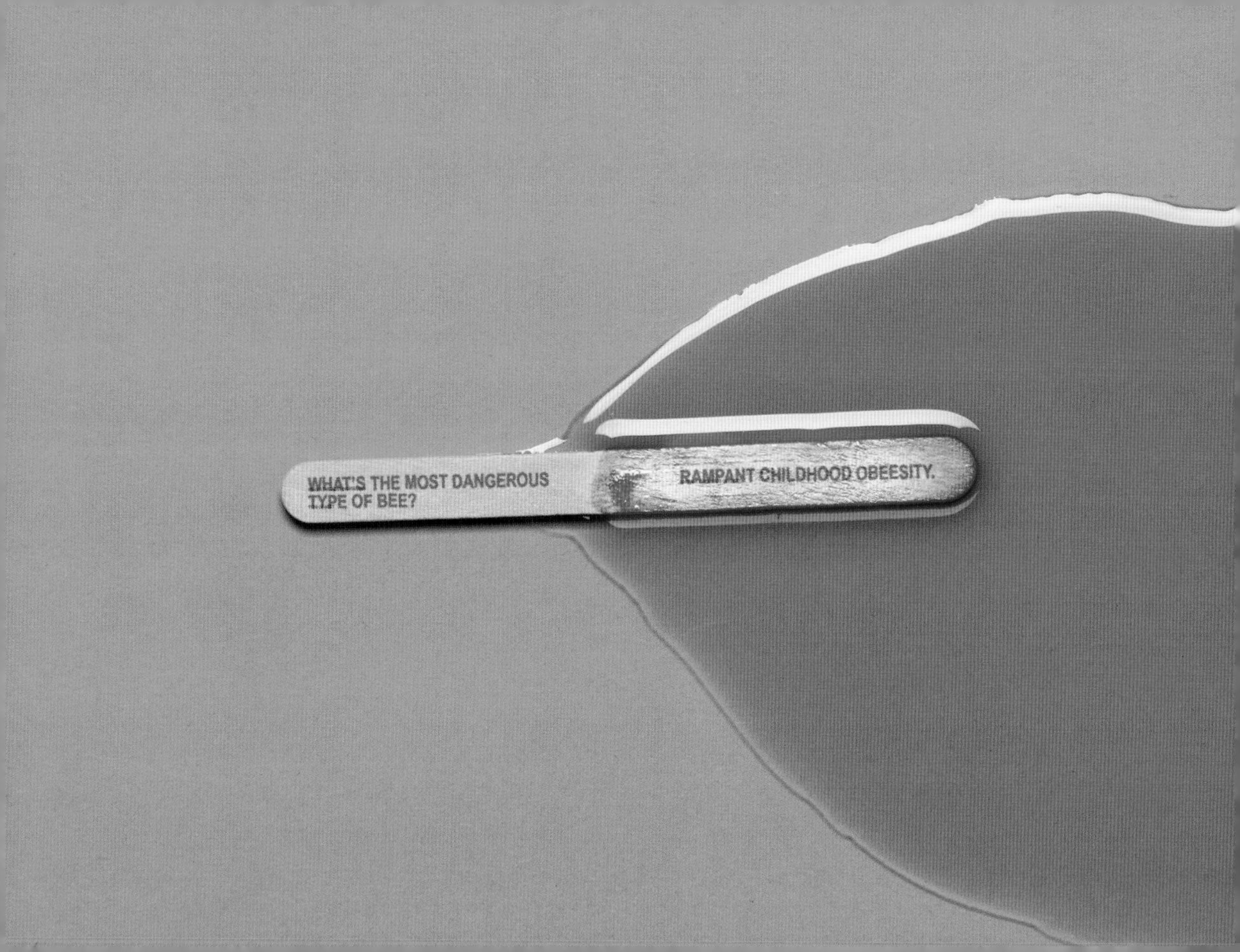
WHAT'S THE MOST DANGEROUS
TYPE OF BEE?
RAMPANT CHILDHOOD OBEESITY.

WHY DID THE BURGLAR
STEAL FROM THE BAKERY?

WHY DID THE BURGLAR
STEAL FROM THE BAKERY?

HE WAS OUT OF OPTIONS.

WHAT DID THE LIBRARIAN
WANT FOR CHRISTMAS?

WHAT DID THE LIBRARIAN WANT FOR CHRISTMAS?

TO BE ABLE TO MAKE LOVE AGAIN.

WHAT KIND OF PILLS DOES
AN OPERA SINGER TAKE?

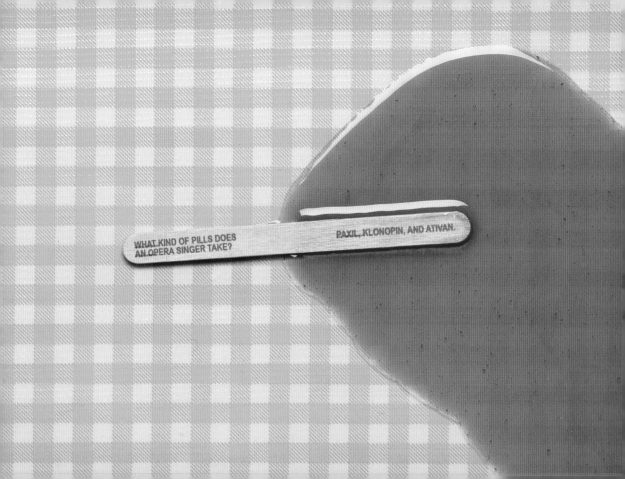

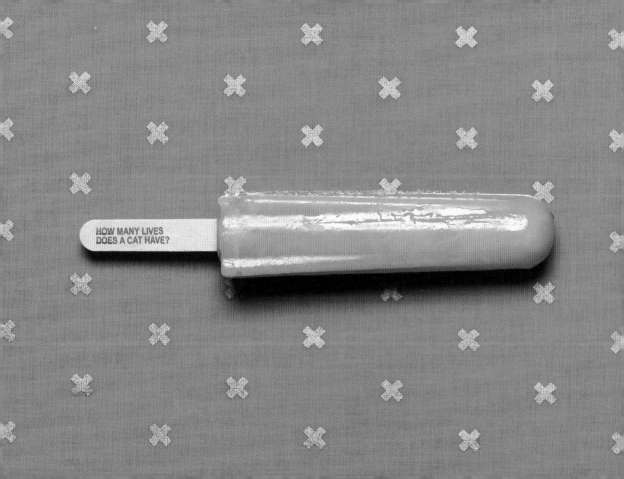

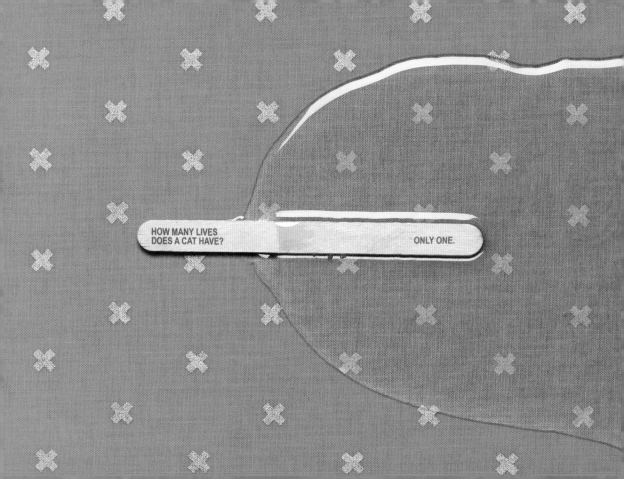

WHY DID THE LIFEGUARD WEAR PANTS?

BECAUSE HE WAS ASHAMED OF HIS BODY.

WHAT DOES A COMEDIAN
DREAM ABOUT?

WHAT DOES A COMEDIAN
DREAM ABOUT?   A REAL JOB.

WHY DID THE BUSINESS-
MAN FLY TO FLORIDA?

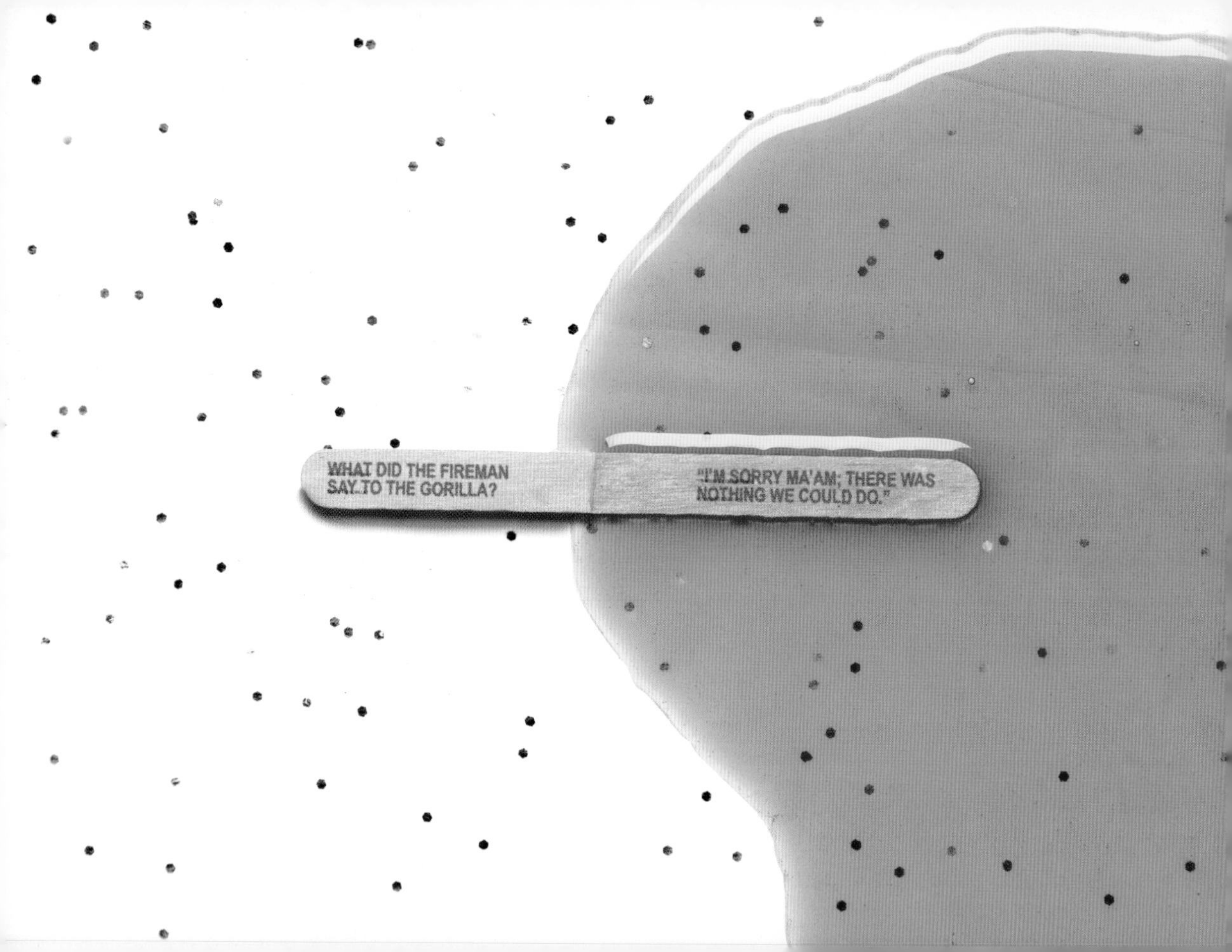
WHAT DID THE FIREMAN
SAY TO THE GORILLA?
"I'M SORRY MA'AM; THERE WAS
NOTHING WE COULD DO."

WHY DID THE CONDUCTOR
STOP THE TRAIN?

WHY DID THE CONDUCTOR
STOP THE TRAIN?

HE JUST NEEDED A MINUTE, OKAY?

WHY WAS THE FISH
UPSET?

HE WAS SUFFOCATING AT THE BOTTOM
OF A DIRTY BOAT.

WHAT KIND OF BOOKS
DO CRIMINALS READ?

WHAT KIND OF BOOKS
DO CRIMINALS READ?

NONE. THEY'RE ILLITERATE!

WHAT DID THE DETECTIVE FIND
ON THE STAIRS?

WHAT DID THE DETECTIVE FIND
ON THE STAIRS?

FLUIDS.

WHY WOULDN'T THE COWBOY
TALK TO THE COWGIRL?

WHY WOULDN'T THE COWBOY
TALK TO THE COWGIRL?

SHE WAS FAT!

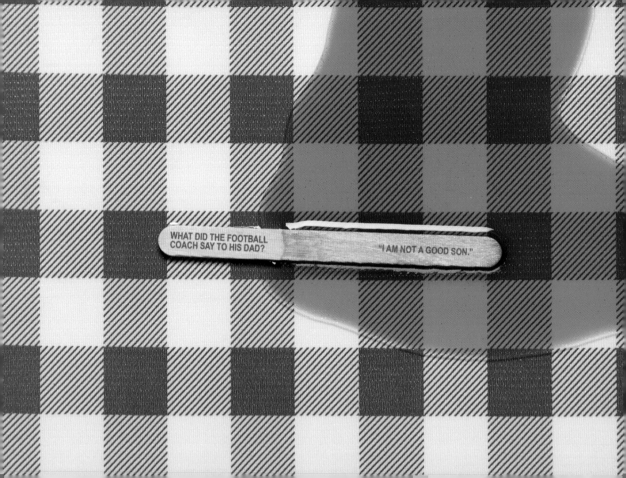

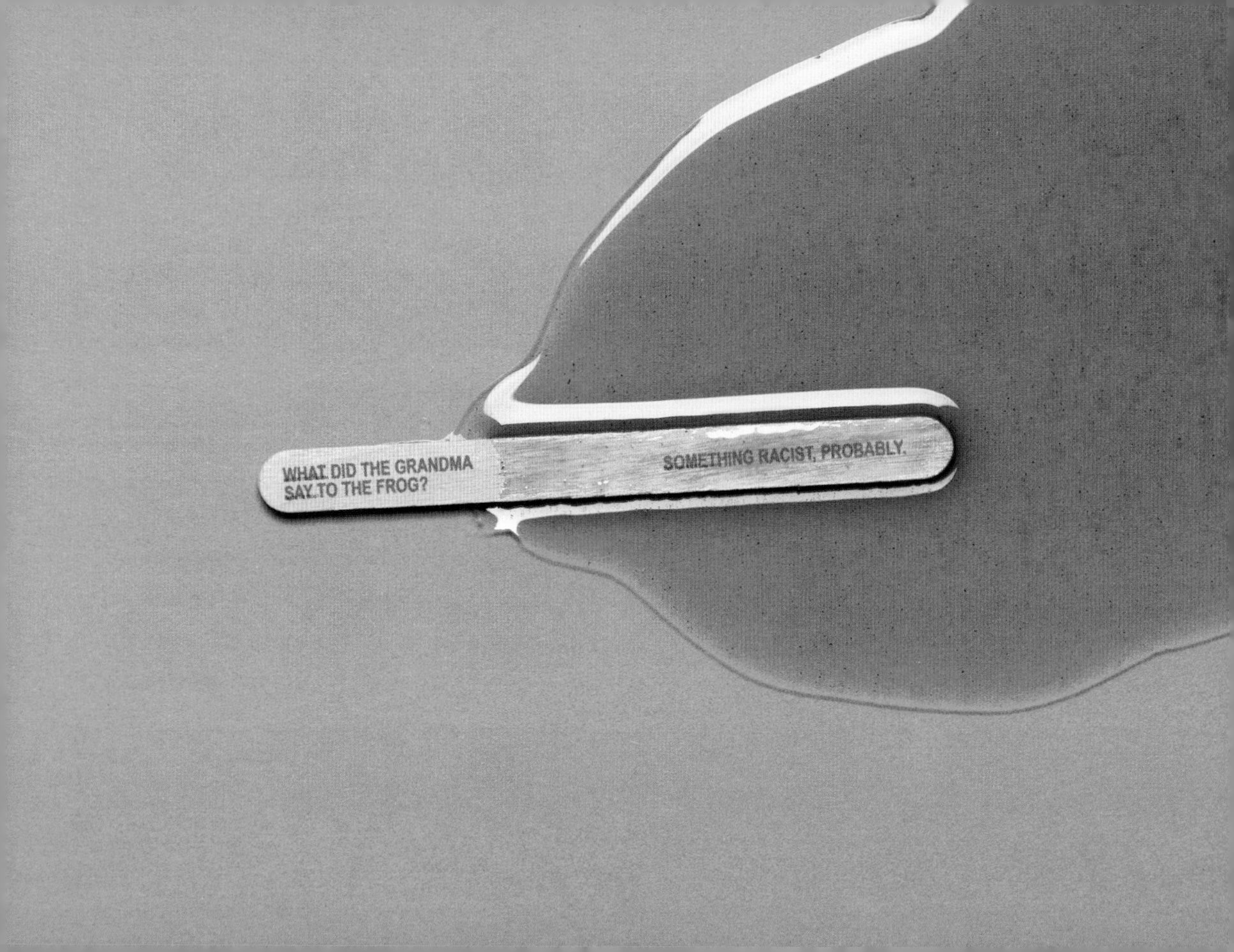
WHAT DID THE GRANDMA SAY TO THE FROG?
SOMETHING RACIST, PROBABLY.

DID YOU HEAR ABOUT THE EXPLOSION AT THE CANDY CORN FACTORY?

YEAH, I THINK LIKE 4 PEOPLE DIED.

WHERE DID THE GOLFER
LOSE HIS BALL?

WHEN IS A HOME NOT
A HOME?

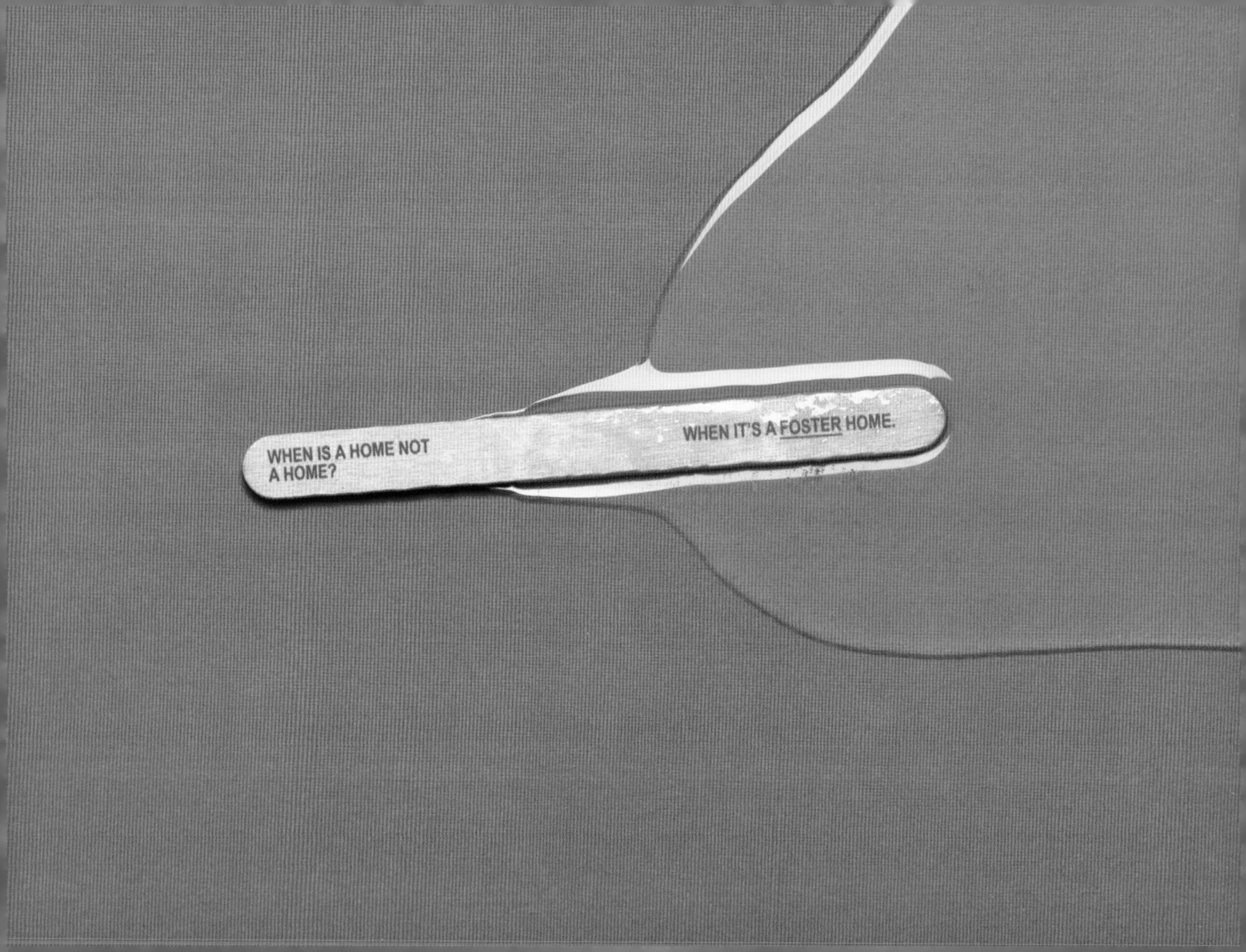
WHEN IS A HOME NOT
A HOME?
WHEN IT'S A FOSTER HOME.

WHY DIDN'T THE GARBAGE
MAN DRIVE A CAR?

WHAT DO YOU CALL
A GOLDFISH WITH BRACES?

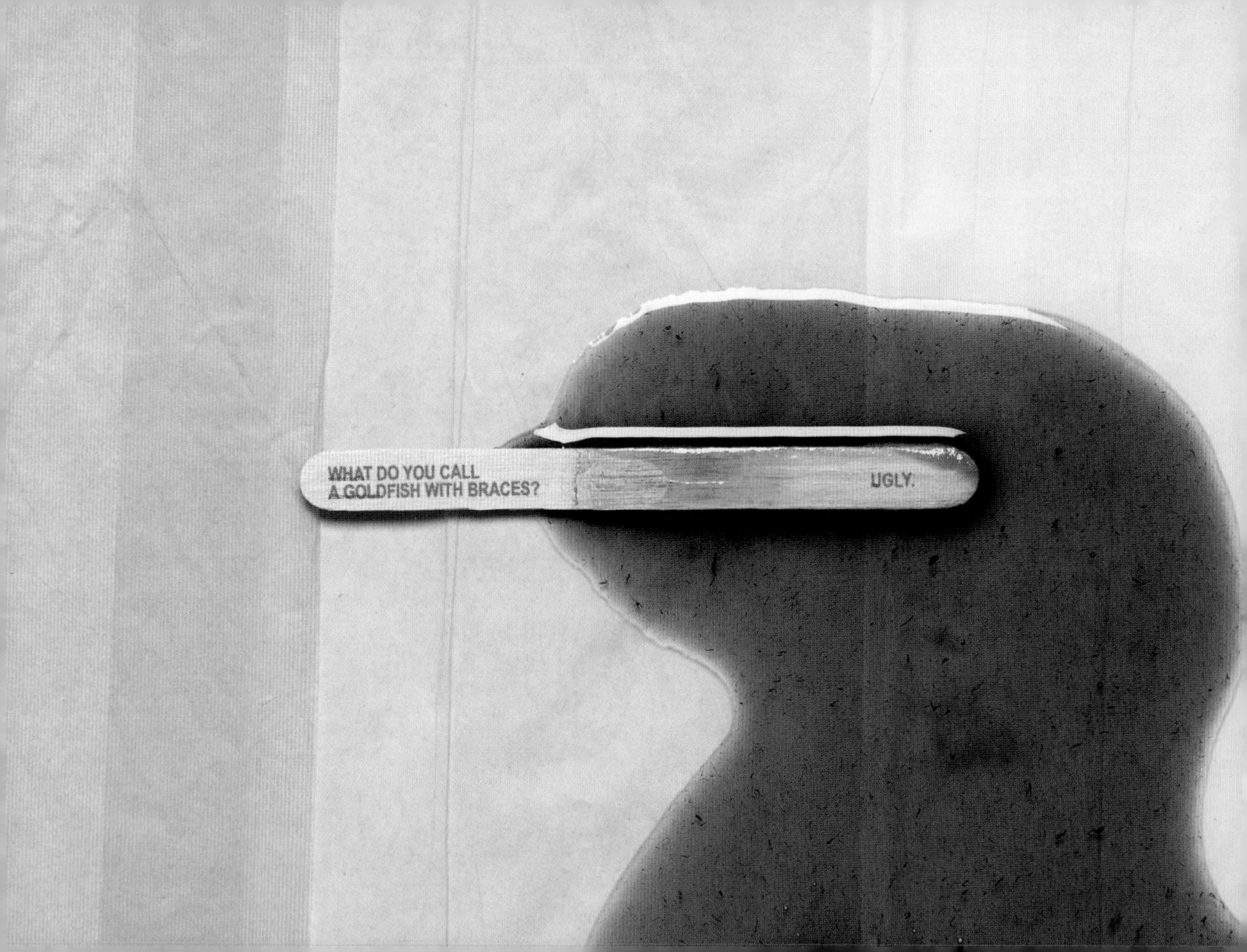
WHAT DO YOU CALL
A GOLDFISH WITH BRACES?
UGLY.

WHAT DID THE SOLDIER FORGET?

WHAT DID THE SOLDIER FORGET?   NOTHING. NOT ONE THING.

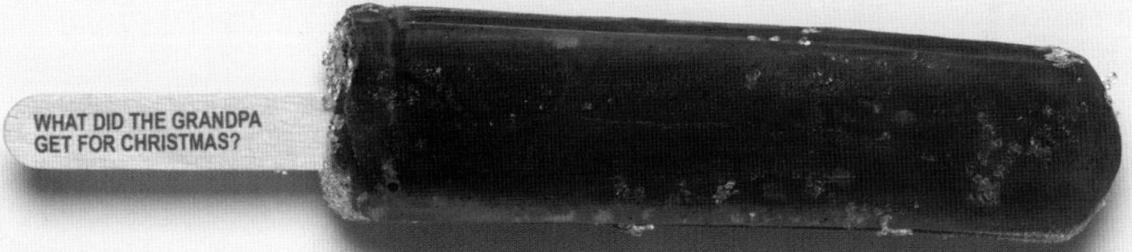
WHAT DID THE GRANDPA
GET FOR CHRISTMAS?

WHAT DID THE GRANDPA
GET FOR CHRISTMAS?

A LITTLE BIT LONELIER.

WHY WAS THE GHOST SAD?

A BUNCH OF DIFFERENT REASONS.

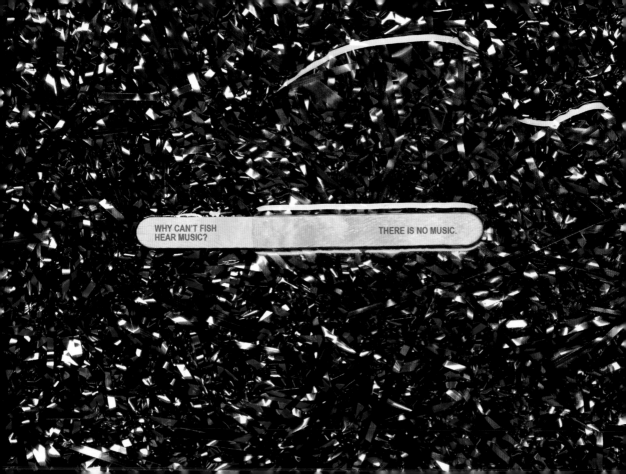

WHY DID THE LAMP IGNORE
THE CHAIR?

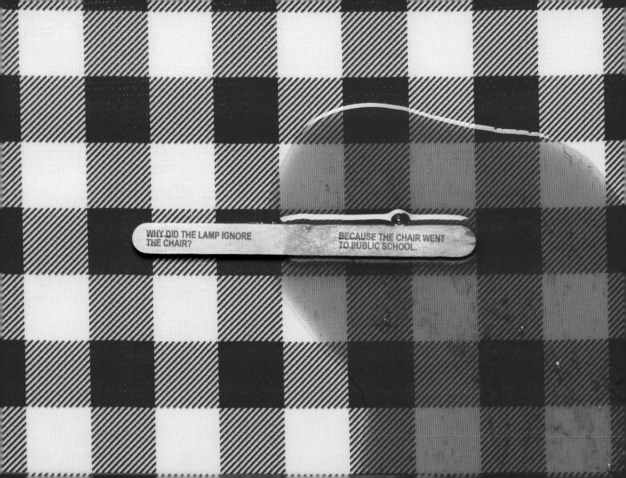

WHY WASN'T THE LADYBUG
INVITED TO DINNER?

SHE WAS JUST KIND OF A BITCH.

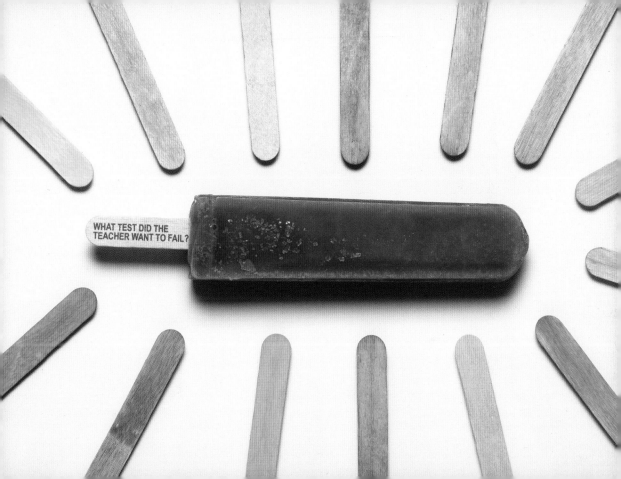

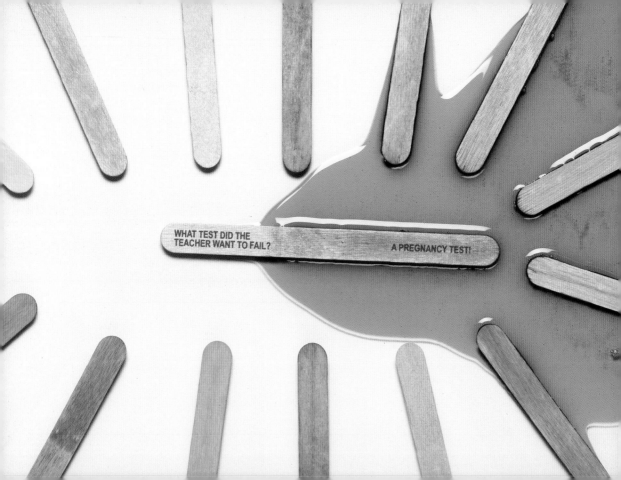

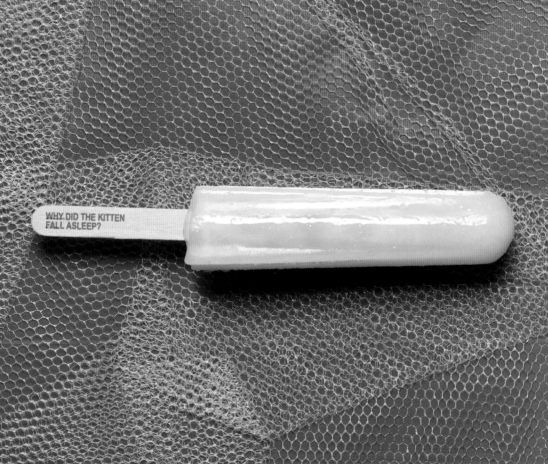

WHY DID THE KITTEN
FALL ASLEEP?

WHY DID THE KITTEN
FALL ASLEEP?

SHE ISN'T ASLEEP, HONEY. SOMETIMES NOT ALL
THE KITTENS MAKE IT OUTSIDE THEIR MOMMY.

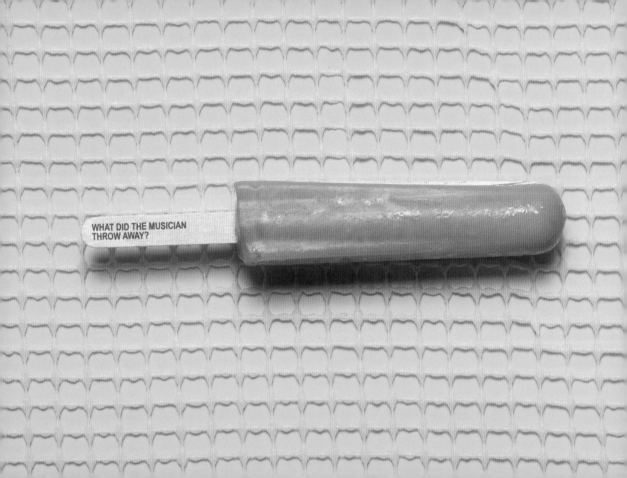

WHAT DID THE MUSICIAN
THROW AWAY?

WHAT DID THE MUSICIAN
THROW AWAY?

HIS FUTURE.

WHY DOES A NURSE
GO TO THE MOVIES?

WHY DOES A NURSE
GO TO THE MOVIES?

TO ESCAPE.

WHERE DOES A REAL ESTATE
AGENT EAT?

WHERE DOES A REAL ESTATE
AGENT EAT?

ALONE AT HER DESK!

WHAT DID THE MAN SAY
TO THE MOVIE STAR?

"GIVE ME YOUR FINGERNAILS. I NEED THEM."

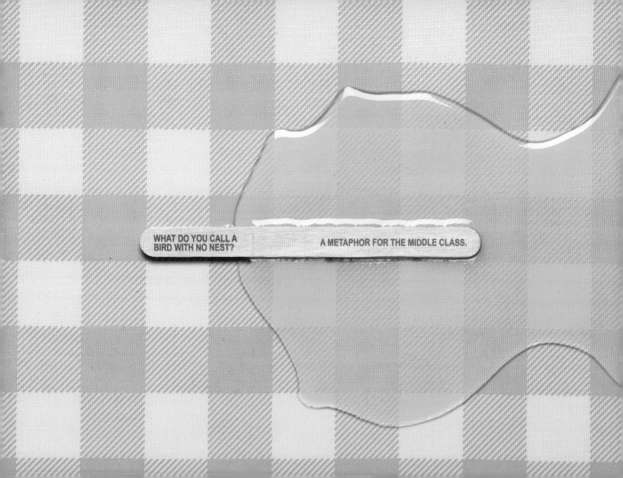

WHAT ARE THE THREE MOST
IMPORTANT LETTERS TO A WAITRESS?

WHAT ARE THE THREE MOST
IMPORTANT LETTERS TO A WAITRESS?

G - E - D

WHY DID THE RIVER CRY?

WHY DID THE RIVER CRY?
BECAUSE TODD REFUSES TO GET THE HELP HE NEEDS.

WHY COULDN'T THE ROCK 'N' ROLL
SINGER PERFORM?

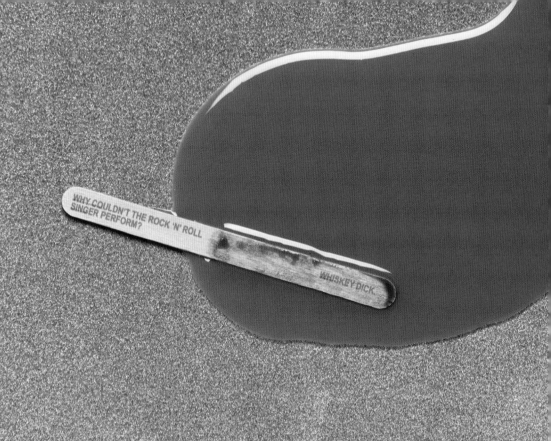

WHAT KIND OF KEY DOES
A STOCKBROKER NEED?

WHAT KIND OF KEY DOES
A STOCKBROKER NEED?

A KEY BUMP!

WHAT DID THE SUNFLOWER SAY TO HER SISTER?

WHAT DID THE SUNFLOWER SAY
TO HER SISTER?   NOTHING, FOR MORE THAN THREE YEARS.

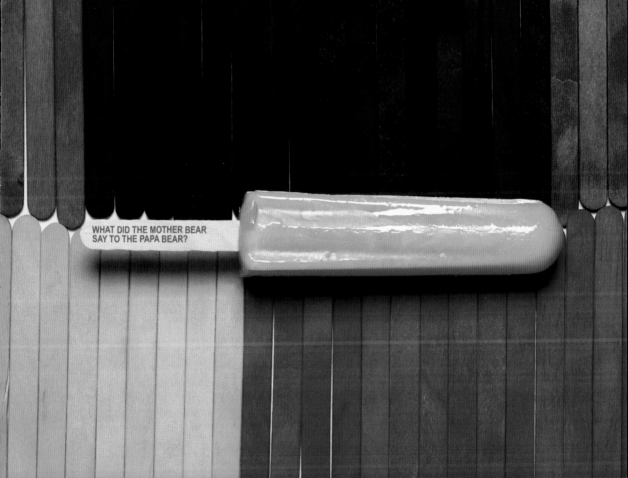

WHAT DID THE MOTHER BEAR
SAY TO THE PAPA BEAR?

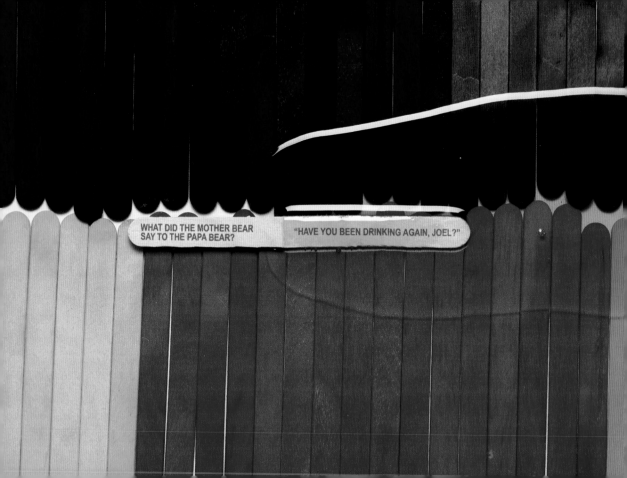

WHAT KIND OF TROLL
LIVES UNDER A BRIDGE?

HOW IS A RECEPTIONIST
LIKE A ROBOT?

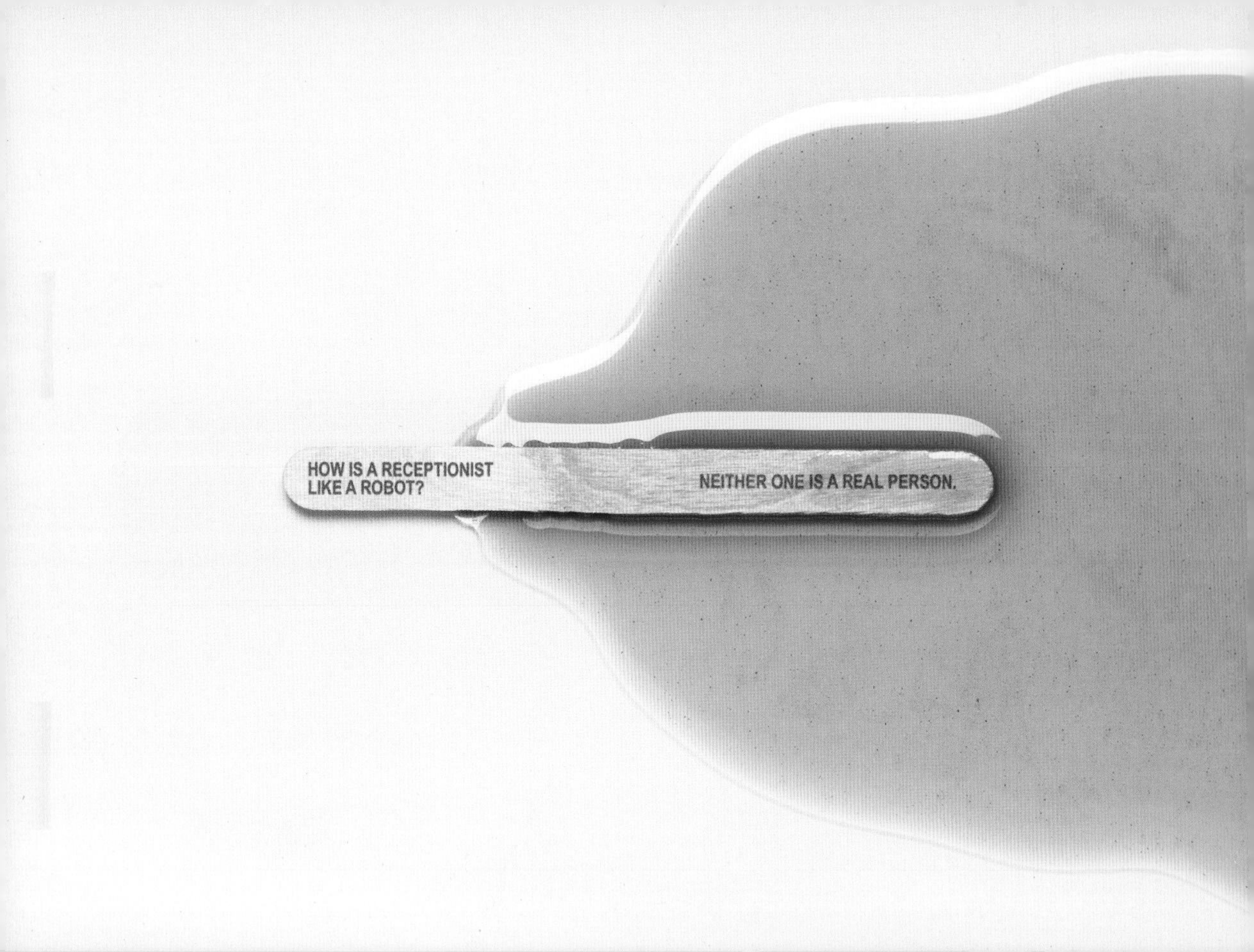
HOW IS A RECEPTIONIST
LIKE A ROBOT?
NEITHER ONE IS A REAL PERSON.

ABOUT THE AUTHORS

Jason Kreher and Matt Moore are advertising coworkers and longtime friends. Jason lives in Portland, Oregon, with his husband Eirik, while Matt lives in Tokyo and is completely alone. This is their first book.

For jokes deemed too offensive to publish, please consider visiting: *www.schadenfreezers.com*.